The 4G Factor

Guts, Grit, and Grind Produce Greatness

By Gretchen D. Barron

Dedication

This book is dedicated to the women who have stood with me from day one. You have been there through EVERY "G." I am who I am in part because of your love and support. THANK YOU!

Table of Contents

Introduction

Hey, Girl!

Thank you for joining me on the journey to greatness. I wrote this book just for you. YES, YOU! It's for the "you" you want to become but are having difficulty getting started. It's you whose life knocked you down. It's you who others told was crazy for dreaming.

I am blessed to be a successful business owner, a local servant-leader, and a mom to two AMAZING boys. This life has been filled with highs and lows, fighting against stereotypes and biases while warring an internal battle for the pursuit of greatness. My pursuit of greatness is not just personal; I want to be a beacon of inspiration for countless others who aspire to be and do more.

In this book, I will use my life as a case study to discuss each of the g's: guts, grit, grind, and greatness. I hope this book will strengthen you to define your path to greatness and develop an unwavering spirit that will carry you through each level, carving trails and breaking barriers.

Remember, grinding is not to pursue your dreams but to achieve the goals that will manifest the dream.

Happy reading,

Gretchen

Section 1

Guts

Chapter 1

Grown Guts

"Gold medals aren't really made of gold. They're made of sweat, determination, and a hard-to-find alloy called guts." — Dan Gable

One of an athlete's greatest accomplishments is winning over their opponents. People may see outward things like championship rings, metals, or trophies, but for the athlete, it's the sweat, pain, blood, and tears. It's the discipline to outwork, strategize, and ultimately beat your opponent. This, my friend, is called guts. Having guts is the difference between winners and those who quit or give up because it's "too hard." Having guts is being able to push past the noise in your head and keep moving despite how you feel or what you see. This is the fight of a true champion willing to overcome all odds and reach their full potential.

To possess the 4G Factor, you must have some key traits, including guts. We often use the word guts to challenge someone, such as "She doesn't have guts!" For the sake of this book, we will use guts as the courage that comes from a personal conviction. That thing inside of you that says there's more. Guts is that thing that tells you to keep going. It separates those who look at the mountain and talk about it from those who look at it, wonder what it's like on the other side, and decide to climb it. Guts is looking at something and not knowing how or why, but without hesitation continues to move forward. Being great comes from long hours, long weeks, extreme highs and lows, and the guts to stick it out. I call this "grown guts."

Grown guts are when you own your journey and know the buck stops with you. The Bible says you make your way prosperous. You move at the risk of being looked at like you have ten heads. (Don't worry, as you settle into the 4G, ten heads don't feel so heavy!) Having grown guts is settling into your responsibility and understanding that you reap all the rewards of success or the consequences of failure. It is the epitome of doing it scared. Afraid of the unknown. Afraid of the what if. But here's a thought: what if it could be good?

I am reminded of one of my first REAL GROWN GUTS MOMENTS. Picture it, Sicily, 2007... (HA! Love the Golden Girls!!!) I was laid off from SC DJJ. I had a consulting business that I had been working on the side, writing grants and doing training. It was my little side hustle. Before I continue with the story, I think it's important to note that for years I walked around saying that I was NOT going to retire from the State Government. I did not know what that looked like, but I knew (as my grandmother would say) deep down in my "knower" that I would not be punching someone's clock for the rest of my life. Now that's some GROWN GUTS!!! I had no plan, but A LOT of confidence.

Now, back to the story. It was decided that I would work in the consulting business and see what happens. So, here I am, laid off from my GOOD PAYING government job, with NO salary and no actual plan, but I had peace. Over several months, I would get a contract here or there, but no "real" money that said, "We are going to be alright." I went to church, and my pastor started a series entitled, "Do It Scared!" He talked about how it may not make sense to nobody but you, but do it scared! It may not initially add up, but do it scared! You may not have seen or heard of it, but do it scared! He said if you have a hope and a promise, hold on to that and don't stop! SLAP YOUR NEIGHBOR HIGH-FIVE AND SAY GROWN GUTS!!! I was pumped and ready to blow the week out of the water. I knew something was going to happen that week. And it did, but it wasn't what I thought it would be.

I had to make a grown guts decision: to get a job or not get a job was the question. I had no money coming into the home from my personal contributions. I agreed to look for work but could NOT get a job for nothing. When I tell y'all Walmart wouldn't hire me, NO ONE! I searched the web every day, but nothing came about. I was so sad and felt useless and worthless. Here I am, a well-educated woman who cannot get a job anywhere.

I remember pulling into our garage one morning after taking our son to school, feeling overwhelmed and inadequate.

Here was this problem that I couldn't seem to fix. When I worked for the state government, I was the go-to person who could create and design successful programs, but I couldn't create or design a thing for myself. I began to cry and feel sorry for myself. I must have sat there for over an hour having a pity party.

My phone rang, and little did I know that my party was getting ready to be bust slam up!!! On the other end of the phone was my Co-Pastor and mentor, who asked, "Hi, Gretchen. How's it going?"

Me: "Fine."

Mentor: "No, really how's it going?"

Me: "It's not." And I began to give her the rundown of everything going on.

Mentor: "Ok, are you finished? So, what are you going to do? Because all I hear is that you have been sitting in the car for the past hour, wasting time that you could have been putting things together for your business. Have you ever thought about what would happen if someone called you today and wanted to hire you as a consultant? Would you be ready to start immediately?"

Boy, she knocked the wind out of my sail fast, quick, and in a hurry. She also told me it's ok to have a moment, but you can't stay there.

> That was the moment I created the "30-second rule". You can trip for 30 seconds, but after 30 seconds, wipe your face, dust yourself off, and remember what God said. Please know I understand some situations may cause you to renew your 30 seconds if you don't get stuck.

I got out of that car, went into the house, and began creating documents and forms for the clients I did not have. Later on, someone asked me what I did that day. Shaking in my boots, I said, "I created business documents." I had decided not to apply for any more jobs and that this *was* my job. GROWN GUTS! I knew then that I was out of the boat, and it was time to walk on water.

You may hear that story and say, Gretchen, I don't think I have guts, let alone grown guts, but I want them. Everyone has guts, but some of us have more developed guts. I liken it to muscles. Everyone has muscles. Some of us work out to strengthen them and bulk up; others do nothing, which determines our strength. Guts is similar to that scenario. Guts are just like muscles. The more you work with them, the stronger they become. It starts with small things like having the guts to say no when you usually say yes, or for me, it was wearing clothing that I would not normally wear.

For example, I LOVVVVVVVE the color orange. (Let me be clear that I am NOT a CLEMSON TiGER! I AM A

PROUD USC GAMECOCK!!!!) I always wanted some orange glasses but wouldn't get any. I would talk myself out of it by saying they cost too much for them not to be practical. Would you believe it when I tell you I opened my email, and there they were, orange glasses for $14!!!! I had no more excuses. Now, all I had to do was purchase them. I called a couple of my girlfriends, asked them, asked the Barron Boys, and everyone was like, "What's the big deal?" So, I did. They came in the mail and sat in the draw for at least two weeks. I finally decided to wear them.

I was so concerned about what others would say because they were so out of character for me. Even though I was worried, baby, let me tell you, I ROCKED those glasses with everything I had in me. The entire evening, I received endless compliments about my glasses. And just like muscle building takes consistent practice to strengthen your body, making courageous, bold moves like wearing orange glasses strengthens your guts. Grown guts are needed to silence all those negative things inside your head. You learned how to think. At some point, something changed your thoughts and turned your guts off. Tell the noise to be quiet or to SHUT UP. It is shaping you into someone who you are not.

Grown Guts Recap

Do it scared!

Remember the 30 second rule.

Plan and create during your downtime.

No turning back, you are out of the boat now!

4G Moment to Reflect

Do you have "grown guts?" Why or why not?

____

____

____

____

Recall a "grown guts" moment. How did it shape who you are today?

____

____

____

____

Chapter 2

Understand and Assess Risk (Make a Plan)

"I know you think you heard what I said but I'm not sure what said is what you heard…" -Author Unknown

I say at least ten times daily, "Why are they looking at me like I have ten heads?" When I start to talk, some people's faces look like they see a purple horse with snakes, elephants, turtles, and bunny rabbits coming out of my head. Ridiculous, right? But is it? It really isn't because everyone does not possess the 4G Factor. When they don't, they will often misunderstand you. People misunderstand me or challenge my words because it causes them to see things from a different perspective. They may NEVER understand because it's hard for pigeons to breathe the air at the altitude where eagles soar. It took me some time to get this because we all want to be heard and understood.

> "It's hard for pigeons to breathe the air at the altitude where eagles soar."

Starting something new is always a risk. Keep in mind there is no guarantee of success, and there is always the possibility of failure. However, taking risks is essential for growth and progress. If we never take risks, we will never achieve anything new.

When starting something new, it is important to understand and assess the risks involved. That means thinking about all the possible outcomes and challenges, both good and bad. It also means being realistic about your abilities and resources. So many people start a new business or project with larger-than-life plans that do not match their skill set or financial and human resources needed to get started, let alone maintain it over a long period. Once you have a good understanding of the risks, you can determine how to proceed.

If you decide to proceed, be prepared for the possibility of failure. That means having a backup plan and being willing to learn from your mistakes. It also means being resilient and not giving up easily. When I started my consulting business, I remember submitting HUNDREDS of proposals and responding to many solicitations only to get a no.

I will be the first to admit that hearing no so many times was hard for me. It was even harder to look at people and say that I was in business but did not have "any business." There was a time when I quit my business every week (I still do this to this day!). It was WAY too hard and uncomfortable, but I would hear Dr. Martin Luther King's quote ring in my ear. It has become my mantra for life!

> *"If you can't fly then run, if you can't run then walk, if you can't walk then crawl, but whatever you do you have to keep moving forward."*

Understanding and assessing risk when starting something new requires you to:

1. Do your research. Learn as much as you can about the industry you are entering and the specific business you are planning to start.

2. Talk to experts. Talk to people who have experience and known success in their area. It doesn't necessarily have to be in your field. You can learn many lessons from successful people that can be applied generally. It's the time to listen and do LITTLE talking. You can avoid many mistakes by sitting at the feet of someone who knows more than you.

3. Create a plan. The first plan is how you plan to execute this project. Start with your implementation plan, steps 1, 2, etc. These are things like meeting with Gretchen Barron to discuss how to apply for government contracts, create website content, and determine the best

web hosting site.

    a. The second plan is a business plan. A business plan will help you to identify and assess the risks involved in your business. It also can be used to secure funds from financial institutions or investors.

4. Create a budget to get your project off the ground. Then, create a budget outlining how you can expand. The best way to set yourself up for success is to unroll your project in phases. It's equivalent to eating an elephant one bit at a time. Having enough funding will help you to weather any storms that come your way. Side note: You should have your own money to invest in YOU before seeking outside sources.

5. Be prepared to work hard. Starting something is a lot of work. Be ready to put in the long hours and make sacrifices.

6. Be patient. Success doesn't happen overnight. Be patient and persistent, and you will eventually achieve your goals.

Starting something new is never easy, but it is always worth it. If you are willing to take risks and work hard, you can achieve anything you set your mind to. It's putting your "grown guts" into action! When you possess the 4G Factor, you must silence the noise inside your head that tells you, you will not succeed. You must risk moving forward if you are the ONLY person who believes in what you are doing. Once you step out of the boat, you must be willing to walk on water at the risk of looking stupid and even being alone. When you face this music, you are ready for Phase 1: Isolation: Stealth Mode.

In today's society, isolation is like a cuss word, but when you are on the brink of what you believe to be life-changing, it's common. It's been my experience to isolate myself to avoid hearing anything contrary to my beliefs. The negativity can impede your progress, and when you are walking on water and the first out of the boat, the last thing you need is to hear someone speaking against the plan that you are eating and breathing day in and day out. Therefore, it's okay to isolate yourself during this time. In fact, it can be beneficial to your productivity and success. When you're first starting something new, it's essential to have time to focus and get your bearings. This can be difficult if you're constantly being interrupted by people or other demands on your time. Isolating yourself can help you block out distractions and give you the time and space to think clearly and work effectively.

I am by no means saying that you must move to a secluded place where only you and God's creatures are well. Of course, it's important to find a balance. You don't want to isolate yourself so much that you become cut off from the world and your support system. But if you can find a way to carve out some time to focus on your work, it can be a great way to get ahead.

Isolation also looks like not talking about what you are doing but working in stealth mode, working underground. For context, stealth mode is operating at a level where you're undetected. It is riding under the radar where the average "Joe Blow" does not suspect anything. Stealth mode is also to protect one's privacy.

While writing this book, I have isolated every fiber about this project. I chose to do this because it took me over five years to write this book because of the negative feedback I received from different people. Also, because it's a season where everyone is writing a book, I did not want ANYTHING to distract or derail my progress. I am deliberate about who I speak to about the 4G Factor. I believe people do not mean any harm, but all it takes is one seed of doubt, and before you know it, your dream has been deferred, and your guts have gone out the door.

Isolating yourself while creating something new can be a great way to get ahead. Make sure you find a balance that works for you, and don't isolate yourself so much that you become cut off from the world and your support system. Starting something new is a risk, but it is a risk that is worth taking. If you are willing to put in the hard work and be prepared for the possibility of failure, you can achieve anything you set your mind to.

It takes guts to start something new. It takes courage to step outside of your comfort zone and take risks. It takes determination to keep going even when things get tough. But the rewards can be great if you are willing to take the risk.

22

4G Moment to Reflect

Use the space below to create a plan to begin to execute your 4G project.

Chapter 3

Encourage Yourself

"Whether you think you can or you think you can't, you're right."
-Henry Ford

Do you believe in yourself? If you don't, it's time to start. Dare to believe in yourself. Believing in yourself is one of the most important things you can do in life. It helps you to achieve your goals, overcome challenges, and live a happy and fulfilling life. Believing in yourself makes you more likely to take risks and try new things. You are also more likely to persevere in the face of setbacks. And you are more likely to achieve your goals. To dare to believe takes GUTS.

When you dare to believe, you are saying you can do anything you set your mind to. You are saying you can achieve your dreams and make a difference. It is what you believe in, not others. It is risking looking crazy, which is why Phase 1 is so important. Because by this time, you have it settled that you will do… NO MATTER WHAT! You have settled that you believe in your project even when it seems impossible to others.

Women who possess the 4G Factor spend many days talking to themselves, encouraging themselves to not quit or give up. This is one of the most essential skills to develop, to dare to believe. It's like an athlete who KNOWS they are GOOD! My youngest son has confidence like I have NEVER seen. You cannot tell this kid that he cannot do anything. You talk about having "heart," he has it! What I love about him is even when he's wavering or has a little doubt, he still speaks with a winner's attitude.

Joyce Myers, minister and author, said that half the battle is in our mind. I totally agree with this. If we can silence the noise in our heads, we can dare to believe in ourselves and our projects. It is about YOU and ONLY YOU! If you need a cheerleader on the sidelines of your life, I can assure you that to possess the 4G Factor, that's probably not going to happen!!!

> **4G people understand that my success, my winning in MY life, is singular, and I am the ONLY person responsible!**

The 4G path can be compared to walking in a tunnel. You can't see what's happening outside the tunnel, but you know something is happening, and you won't stop until you get out. While working to get out of the tunnel as quickly as possible, you know it's a long path with unforeseen circumstances. To maximize your full potential, you must dare to believe it won't be long before you come out of the tunnel.

Why is it important to believe in yourself?

- When you believe in yourself, you are more likely to take action. You are more likely to set goals and go after them.

- When you believe in yourself, you are more likely to persevere when facing challenges. You are more likely to keep going even when things get tough.

- When you believe in yourself, you are more likely to achieve your goals. You are more likely to reach your full potential.

Living the 4G Factor is a lot of work and requires you to live a happy and fulfilling life. It requires you to dare to believe, and take the necessary steps:

- Set goals and go after them,
- Define what success looks like,
- Don't give up on your dreams/plans,
- Examine your thoughts and habits,
- Don't settle,
- Surround yourself with positive people,
- Be kind to yourself,
- Take care of yourself physically and mentally.

4G life can be intense, and taking care of yourself is essential. There is nothing worse than being too tired to enjoy or celebrate what you have worked so hard for. I remember when I ran for public office in the midst of COVID-19. The fact that I had NO clue what I was doing was one thing, but running for office during a global pandemic was another. My being an overachiever and type A personality didn't help at all. I ate, breathed, and ran for office. People would tell me, Gretchen, you must take a break. Do you think I did? NOOOOO!

Fast forward to election night, there was chaos at just about all precincts, and the results did not come in until early morning. When I received the news that I was in a runoff, I was so drained that I had NOTHING to celebrate. I was so focused on winning that I failed to take care of myself so that I could enjoy the process. Spirituality, self-help, and self-care are all important aspects of life. They are especially important when creating something new. A strong sense of purpose and motivation is essential when working on that new thing.

Spirituality can help you to connect with your higher power and find inspiration. When you feel lost or discouraged, connecting with your higher power can give you the strength to keep going. What does it look like? For me, it's attending weekly women's Bible study. This is a space specifically for women where I gain strength to tackle what I face as a woman, mom, business owner, and servant leader.

Self-help can help you to develop the skills and knowledge you need to be successful. Many books, articles, and websites can teach you about project management, marketing, and other essential skills. Invest in your future. Subscribe to journals, attend conferences, and watch YouTube videos. Please do not underestimate YouTube for self-help. I spend endless hours watching and listening to videos on various topics. This also looks like mentorship. I mentioned in the previous chapter to connect with someone who has already dug ground out and has proven successful. My Pastor said this: "Sow where you want to go." Connect with someone who has achieved the things you desire. I'm going to put a pin right here…

Side Note: I'm writing this book to share my insight because I have not had many people willing to mentor or share information and insight. This is especially a big deal in the African-American community when it comes to women. I want to take this opportunity to encourage you to commit to reaching back and helping another woman after you make it to your place of success.

> **It's lonely at the top because we do not take anyone with us!**

Self-care can help you to stay healthy and balanced during the challenging times that inevitably come with any new project. Make sure to get enough sleep, eat healthy foods, and exercise regularly. It is also important to take time for yourself to relax and de-stress. Starting something new takes a toll on your ENTIRE body. I know running through a drive-thru is easier, but it's not good for you. BABBBBBBBBBEEEE, LISTEN, I am talking to myself right here and right now! I am GUILTY of going through a particular drive-thru getting a large fry and Pepsi, no ice. NOT GOOD for you or me. We must be deliberate and make healthy eating choices, especially on a 4G path.

Another point is to get plenty of rest. This is unusually hard in the 4G life, but it is NEEDED. If you stay up late, try to stay on your same morning schedule but have a short day or take a midday nap to refresh yourself. One thing that works for me if my schedule doesn't permit me to have a nap or early day is that I take minibreaks, play ocean waves (I LOVE the beach. It's my happy place) and unplug for 15 minutes or so. So REFRESHING! I recently incorporated quarterly spa days to recharge.

Lastly, find someone to talk to. This is someone who you can debrief and declutter with. I have found this keeps my stress level down. If you don't have someone to talk to personally, consider going to a therapist. This has been LIFE CHANGING for me!

If you are working on a new project, I encourage you to incorporate spirituality, self-help, and self-care into your process. These practices can help you to stay focused, motivated, and healthy during the journey.

4G Moment to Reflect

What are 3 things you will do to promote self-care, self-help, and spirituality in your personal life?

Chapter 4

Get Use to Being Uncomfortable

Getting comfortable with being uncomfortable is one of the most important things you can do in life. It's what allows you to grow, learn, and take risks. When you're constantly comfortable, you never push yourself outside your comfort zone. You're never learning anything new or challenging yourself.

But being uncomfortable can be scary. It can be hard to step outside your comfort zone and try new things. But it's worth it. When you do, you'll be surprised at your capabilities.

Celebrate your successes. When you do something that makes you uncomfortable, celebrate. This will help you build confidence and make it easier to do things that make you uncomfortable in the future.

Getting comfortable with being uncomfortable is a process. It takes time and effort. But it's worth it. You'll be amazed at what you achieve.

Starting on a new project often entails stepping into the unknown, where uncertainty and discomfort hang out. However, it is within these moments of discomfort that creativity thrives, and skill building is cultivated. Being ok with being uncomfortable is the importance of embracing starting a new project fostering growth, innovation, and personal development.

The journey of creating something new is wrapped up with uncertainty. It's natural to feel discomfort when faced with unfamiliar challenges or when venturing outside of one's comfort zone. However, rather than shying away, it is crucial to embrace it. Embracing uncertainty opens the door to new possibilities and pushes you to explore uncharted territories, leading to innovation and breakthroughs. I like to say that you are tapping into your 4G.

If you want to see me turn up my 4G, tell me it can't be done or there's a problem that needs to be solved. My Mama loves tell stories about me growing up and usually ends the story with you would have to kill Gretchen if you told her she couldn't do something.

> **Creativity blossoms in the face of adversity.**

When confronted with an uncomfortable situation, 4G people will automatically adapt, go into problem-solving mode, and think outside the box. This cultivates resilience—the ability to bounce back from setbacks and persevere in the face of challenges. By learning to navigate through discomfort, you develop the resilience needed to overcome obstacles and achieve their goals.

Embracing discomfort is a sign of a growth mindset—a belief that abilities can be developed through dedication and hard work. Instead of viewing being comfortable as a bad thing or a roadblock, those living in the 4G life see it as an opportunity for growth and learning. They understand that grasping a particular skill is not going to happen overnight but is the result of continuous effort and persistence. By adopting a growth mindset, you can harness the power of discomfort to propel their creative endeavors forward.

Comfort breeds complacency, while discomfort fuels innovation. When you become too comfortable in their routines, you risk stagnation and mediocrity. On the other hand, embracing discomfort pushes creative boundaries and encourages experimentation. It encourages you to challenge your assumptions, think critically, and explore new ideas. By pushing past your comfort zones, you can unlock their full creative potential and produce work that is truly groundbreaking.

One of my first major projects after being elected to office was to secure funding to refurbish a tennis court in my district. After the ribbon cutting, I noticed a group of beautiful, physically fit women wearing some really cute tennis outfits approaching me. They came over to thank me for assisting with this project. We began to talk about tennis, and they challenged me to learn the game. I told them I would most definitely learn the game if it made me look like them. Fast forward to three years later, I started lessons. I knew nothing about the game, and with every move, I felt like I looked crazy. The swings were uncomfortable and challenging, but I knew I had to keep going if I was going to learn the game. I am PRESENTLY putting myself in an uncomfortable situation to learn the game of tennis. If you are going to possess the 4G Factor, you have to risk looking crazy and get used to being uncomfortable.

You have to create a habit of pushing yourself to your limit, so you know what it is like to be outside of your comfort zone. Over time, you will experience an increased tolerance for discomfort because you have become desensitized. Constantly facing new difficult situations and learning from yourself will strengthen you.

I was talking with someone about this topic, and they asked me what the difference is between "doing it scared" and being comfortable with being uncomfortable. Being uncomfortable is when you are in a situation where things are unfamiliar, unpredictable, and out of your comfort zone. While on the other hand, being scared implies fear or anxiety about something dangerous happening.

You can be uncomfortable without being scared. You can't avoid being uncomfortable. It is a normal part of life that can't be avoided. Being uncomfortable is what you are experiencing if you are considering something new. Over time, you get used to it and move throughout your day without thinking about it.

Embracing being uncomfortable is essential for anyone embarking on a new creative project or for those wanting to live in 4G. It is during this time that you can cultivate resilience, foster a growth mindset, and push your 4G boundaries. By learning to embrace uncertainty and lean into this, you can unlock your full potential, achieve mastery in your craft, and create work that leaves a lasting impact. So, the next time you find yourself faced with discomfort, embrace it as a sign that you are on the right path toward creative growth and innovation.

4G Moment to Reflect

List 2 takeaways from this chapter you plan to implement, and write your implantation strategy below.

____

____

____

____

____

____

____

____

____

____

____

____

____

____

____

____

Section 2

Grit

Chapter 5

Face Obstacles Eyeball to Eyeball

As I approach my fourth year as a servant-leader known to most as a politician or elected official, I have learned that if you want to get things done, you have to work with those who may have opposing views from yours. Opposing views do not make them the devil or the enemy. It merely means that we see things differently. For you to maximize your full potential, you must grasp this skill. IT will help you move at a whole different level. As an African-American woman, this is a skill that MY "Sista" works on. I don't have to agree with you on everything, and we can still be cool, go to dinner, and get things done. But for whatever reason, "we" take it personally if someone challenges us or has a different opinion. It comes across like how dare you have a brain and actually think. "Sista," we make our differences work for both of us. We can discuss our differences cordially and develop a consensus without rolling our necks, getting loud, and mad. We can agree to disagree and move on.

One of my favorite movies is "Lean on Me." Mr. Clark and Dr. Napier, who is Clark's boss but are very close friends, were having an intense conversation about the strategies Dr. Clark was using at his school. Dr. Napier thought they were extreme and unwarranted. While Mr. Clark totally disagrees. After a few rounds of back and forth, Dr. Napier decided how they would handle the situation. Then he said, "Come on, and let's get something to eat." While the conversation was a little more expressive than I would have preferred, it was realistic. Although things got heated, the mission was accomplished.

Working with the opposition is necessary when possessing the 4G Factor. You will always encounter people who disagree with you, whether personally or at work. This group usually thinks your project or new thing is the worst idea ever. How you handle these disagreements can make a big difference in your relationships and success.

In a traditional setting, remember everyone has different perspectives. Try to understand what they are saying and where they are coming from. Be willing to compromise, and don't always try to get your way. Be willing to give and take and find a solution for everyone involved. But this is NOT that kind of party. When creating on the 4G level, you don't have time to convince people what you are doing or why. My boys and I have a saying, "We don't talk about it; we be about it." Simply put, there is no time to spend much time talking and sharing what you are doing with others. Remember, 4G is not a standard skillset; therefore, it takes a special person to understand. I want to prepare you for the moment when you are excited about something with your project and want to share the news. The person you share it with has 50 questions and tries to convince you that you are going down the wrong road. This will happen more often than not. This person or persons will have NO idea about what you are doing but have anointed themselves as the Chief Apostle over your project. While you are ready to go toe to toe with them, don't do it! It's important to be respectful of other people's opinions. Even if you disagree with someone, there's no need to be rude or condescending. Remember that everyone is entitled to their opinion, making a healthy debate. 4G people very seldom burn bridges.

Please understand that I am not saying to be a pushover or a punk. There will be those times when you need to confront issues, but even in those times, my Bishop would say to leave others thinking about their behavior, not yours. Finally, it's important to be positive. Working with opposition can be challenging but also an opportunity to learn and grow. If you approach it with a positive attitude, you'll be more likely to find a solution that works for everyone.

You must get used to opposition or the pushback you will get for thinking differently. It's the people who thought differently or were labeled weird as a child who have great success as adults. I remember when growing up there was A bank that had a commercial with a black sheep walking around white sheep singing, "I'm different and don't care who knows it. Something about me is not the same…". Be okay with being the black sheep or the different person in a group. If you stick with what you've already been doing, you will only accomplish what you have already done. 4G is for people who replace norms with new thoughts and ideas. These thoughts and ideas can challenge the mindset of those around you, whether it is your family, friends, or community.

Those who think differently don't see it as an activity or need inspiration; it's a subconscious, daily habit affecting every area of their lives. This level of thinking challenges the color in the lines of thinking. Sometimes, it feels like you are a rebel or disruptive. Be ok with being a disruptor.

> **4G people color outside of the lines. Do you know why? We don't see lines.**

We see blank pages as a space for us to create. We are the equivalent of giving a child a bucket of legos, and the teacher says make me something. We may be stumped for a while but would have created something in time. While others are in awe of your creation, you are looking at it, trying to figure out how we can make it better.

Stop worrying about that small fraction who are questioning you. They are a part of your assignment. They are confidence builders. They allow you to sharpen your skills. The more opposition you have or, the more others don't understand your project, it is confirmation that God is for you!

4G Moment to Reflect

What are some of the obstacles you need to face?

____

____

____

____

What does "color outside of the lines" mean to you? How does this apply to the way you create?

____

____

____

____

Chapter 6

Stay Confident and Optimistic

Starting a new project can be daunting, but staying confident and optimistic is important. Remember, this is YOUR project, YOUR dream, NO ONE else's! Although you may have cheerleaders along the way, it is solely up to you to stay on track and KNOW that "this thing" will happen. You must remain optimistic and confident at the risk of looking stupid. You probably should not share anything about your new project initially unless it is with a TRIED-and-TRUE individual. This is someone like a mentor, close relative, or friend known for motivating and supporting you. People don't mean any harm, but the slightest bit of sarcasm can plant seeds of doubt. Before you know it, you will have talked yourself out of doing that thing. Those about the 4G life must determine and commit to a direction, pivoting when necessary. Once you determine a direction, staying focused and motivated is easier.

This book is a prime example of the point that I'm making. For over six years, I have been procrastinating in writing this book. When I shared with someone that I was going to write a book that I believed to be transformative for women leaders, the person told me that no one would buy my book. They told me I didn't have enough experience to tell someone anything. This was a dream crusher moment for me. Besides being absolutely mean and hurtful, it planted a seed of doubt that prolonged my writing of this book. Even while writing this sentence, I have to stay confident and optimistic. For every word I type, I tell myself, "Gretchen Barron, this book is going to transform women's lives. Don't stop sharing your story. Someone needs to hear this."

I visualize everything. While I'm having a conversation with someone, I am visualizing what is being said. At this stage in my life, I have found this strategy extremely helpful. I have taken this a step further, and now, instead of just visualizing conversations, I visualize my success. I visualize myself successfully completing whatever that thing is that I am working on. In this case, it is completing this book. I see myself at book signings, speaking to women, and conducting seminars. This will help me to stay motivated and focused. Stop what you are doing right now and visualize yourself doing "that thing" that pushes you to 4G status. What do you see? How do you feel? What are the next steps? Who do you need to talk to? What resources are required? Are there any areas that you can improve on?

I'm sure you have heard, "How do you eat an elephant?" You eat it one bite at a time. In other words, you break that big thing down into small pieces. This is also a great strategy when creating a 4G-level project. Break down your project into smaller tasks. This will make it seem less daunting and more manageable. In his book, *The 7 Habits of Highly Effective People*, Sean Covey teaches to begin with the end in mind. While I TOTALLY agree with this habit, this habit can send you to a place that could stress you out because you see what the end is supposed to be, but it is not where you are presently.

> **My pastor often says that God did not give you a vision to drive you crazy, but He gave it to you to drive you.**

This is one of the hardest things to put in perspective because you know what "that thing" is supposed to be. Instead of trippin' because your project has not fully developed into "that thing," try focusing on one thing at a time. Break it down into smaller parts and then develop it from there. As you complete those small tasks, celebrate your successes. No matter how small, take some time to celebrate your accomplishments. This will help you stay positive and motivated.

Lastly, if you are stumped, ask for help when needed. There's no shame in asking for help when you're struggling. Many people will help you if you ask and want to see you succeed. I will also say that some people will not help you. Don't let those people discourage you. That merely means that they are not the one, and you must look for another.

When I started my business, I called many local business owners for advice or help with simple tasks, and only one person VOLUNTARILY assisted me. This person owned a tax preparation company and was highly successful. She called me one day out of the blue, and we talked for hours. She prayed with me and helped me set attainable goals. To this day, I consider her one of my trusted, tried, and true in my life. She helped push me to 4G status. Thank you, my friend. I will never forget how you helped me!   !

Every now and then, things don't work out like we planned them. This doesn't mean you have to "roll with the punches." This means it's time to bob and weave. This is an opportunity to learn and grow; you can overcome any obstacle and achieve your goals. Those who possess the 4G Factor are fighters, they tend to be very bold and different.

According to Success magazine, the definition of bob and weave is "to make rapid bodily movements up and down and from side to side, for example as an evasive tactic by a boxer." Joe Frazier was known for his powerful left hook and ability to wear his opponent down relentlessly by using the bob and wave tactic. Just like Fraizer, we must be relentless when things change.

Committing to a plan is essential for success in any endeavor. When you have a plan, you have a clear path to follow. You know what you need to do and when you need to do it. This can help you stay on track and avoid making costly mistakes.

Of course, no plan is perfect. Things will inevitably go wrong along the way. But if you are committed to your plan, you will be more likely to overcome these challenges and achieve your goals.

Committing to a plan can be challenging. But it is essential for success. If you can stay committed to your plan, you will be more likely to achieve your goals. Be detail-oriented (meticulous). This will help you avoid costly mistakes and ensure your project is well-executed.

Being detail-oriented is essential for success in any project. When you are detail-oriented, you can pay attention to the small things and ensure that everything is done correctly. This is important in any project but vital in new projects.

When you are starting a new project, there are a lot of things to think about. You must devise a plan, gather resources, and delegate tasks. It is easy to get overwhelmed by all of this, but staying focused and paying attention to the details is important.

One way to stay detail-oriented is to create a checklist of tasks that must be completed. This will help you track your progress and ensure that nothing falls through the cracks. I love to make lists. It gives me a full picture of what I need to do. While I must admit, I HATE paper and most of my life is paperless EXCEPT for me having a journal to make my list. This is the part of my life where old school and new school meet.

Another important tip for being detail-oriented is to double-check your work. Once you complete a task, take some time to review it carefully. Make sure that everything is correct and that there are no errors. This may seem like a waste of time, but it can save you a lot of headaches in the long run.

Being detail-oriented is a skill that takes time and practice to develop. But it will pay off if you are willing to put in the effort. Being detail-oriented makes you more likely to produce high-quality work and avoid costly mistakes. So, if you are starting a new project, pay attention to the details. It will make all the difference. Nothing upsets me more than sending a message that I read over, and it still has a mistake in it when I send it. This drives me crazy! It is also a gentle reminder that we aren't perfect, and we are striving for excellence not perfection.

Perfect the Bob and Weave. This is a technique for dealing with setbacks and challenges. When things don't go according to plan, don't give up. Instead, take a step back, assess the situation, and make a plan to move forward. Bob and weaving is a term used to describe the process of trial and error when creating a new project. It is important to be willing to try new things and be flexible when things don't go according to plan. It is also important to be confident in your abilities and be willing to learn from your mistakes.

In the world of the global pandemic, we called it "pivoting." When I decided to run for office, I announced ONE YEAR before the election. Many thought that this was a bit much, but I knew that this was something I needed to do. As my Grandmother would say, "I an unction from the Lord!" So I did it at the cost of looking stupid to others, and then there was March 15, 2020. The Governor of South Carolina held a press conference stating that schools and pretty much everything but grocery stores would be closed for two weeks. This was also ONE day before I was going to officially file to run for County Council. Two weeks turned into two months, and two months turned into pivoting and running a campaign from my computer. Our entire campaign plan was down the drain because traditional campaigning was not an option. We took the original plan and spiced it up to work for where we were. The pandemic was a punch to the face, but we shook off the hit, adjusted, recreated, and continued. Bob and weave became a way of life during this time because we had to adjust to what the medical professionals recommended for the best way to interact with people.

As a result of learning how to bob and weave, I gained these strategies that I now use regularly:

1. Try new things. Experiment with different things and go with what works best.

2. Adjust and monitor. Master the art of being flexible.
3. Stay confident and optimistic no matter what you see around you.
4. Learn from your mistakes and use them to improve your future projects.

Bob and weaving can be a great way to create successful projects. By being willing to try new things, being flexible, being confident, and being willing to learn from your mistakes, you can overcome any obstacle and achieve your goals.

4G Moment to Reflect

Stop what you are doing right now and visualize yourself doing "that thing" that pushes you to 4G status.

What do you see?

____

____

____

____

How do you feel?

____

____

____

____

What are your next steps?

____

____

____

____

Who do you need to talk to?

____

____

____

____

What resources are required?

____

____

____

____

Are there any areas that you can improve on?

____

____

____

____

Chapter 7

Choose Behaviors of a Winner

The mistake many people make in life is that they try to achieve perfection. Do you want to know what the problem with this is? No one is perfect. It's a misconception. When striving for perfection, you set goals that are unrealistic and impossible to reach. In return, you never feel satisfied. I would instead strive for excellence. Excellence sets you apart from all the others. It focuses on achieving greatness, brilliance, and distinction.

I can hear you saying, "I can't tell the difference between the two." Let's slow this down and take a closer look. The difference between perfection and excellence is that you understand that you may make mistakes along the way and learn from them. On the other hand, with perfection, you never admit weakness and fail to see that things may need to be tweaked or improved. Perfectionists struggle with self-improvement because they do not see anything wrong with their actions. While the world is learning from their mistakes and gleaning from others, perfectionists are busy being great in their own minds.

I've boiled down being excellent to three main things:

1. Focus on your progress.

2. Applaud yourself for what you have accomplished thus far.

3. Measure yourself against yourself.

Focus on your progress.

Perfection will make you think that you haven't accomplished anything. Once you decided to start that thing, progress was already in motion. Perfection will have you chasing an unrealistic bar and believing that you should be further ahead than you are. Focus on what you have achieved and your progress, not what you haven't. What have you accomplished? Where were you 6 months ago? You have done something that others would say is impossible. So, who cares about what you haven't done?

Applaud yourself for what you have accomplished thus far.

Results are important. But if you focus only on results, you will feel inadequate, as if you aren't progressing. Instead, applaud yourself for what you have accomplished thus far. I don't care if it's something as small as researching website prices or making cold calls to potential clients. If you worked to make any progress towards your goals, applaud yourself. Earlier in the book, I said that those of us in these 4G Factors must encourage ourselves and be our #1 cheerleader. Girl, you are killing it! Go ahead, stand up, and give yourself a standing ovation!!! That's right, its ok to talk to yourself. The 4G world can sometimes be lonely so get comfortable with being your best friend and talking to yourself. Don't worry studies show that highly intelligent people talk to themselves so consider yourself in an elite group.

Measure yourself against yourself.

Don't look at other people and think you aren't good enough. Measure yourself against yourself. DO NOT compare yourself to anyone. Their success is for motivation, not measurement. This should not make you feel inadequate. If someone is ahead of you, look at this person and tell yourself that you, too, can achieve what they have and greater, AND you WILL. Your thing is not a duplicate but unique with its own goals. Your thing is your thing; therefore, you should not try to achieve someone else's success. Your 4G project has its own DNA and cannot be duplicated, so why measure yourself against anything but yourself.

> **Sidenote: You need to be educated about your competitors, but you do not need to let that be your driving focus.**

When I ran for office, there were 3 of us vying for the seat. One was the 20-year incumbent, and the other was a community member who appeared well-liked by MANY.

During the campaign's early stages, I would run into either one or both at community meetings. I would hear them talk about certain issues that made me feel like I didn't have a handle on the problems. My team would remind me, saying, "Gretchen, do you!" Later on, after the pandemic, I became concerned because if I had a 20x20 sign, one of them would get a billboard. My team sat me down this time and said, "Gretchen, you have to RUN YOUR RACE. Stop worrying about what they are doing and focus on what we are doing. RUN YOUR RACE!!!"

You can run your race in so many ways. Here are a few:

- Execute your plan
- Do your work, not someone else's
- Do you, Boo
- Worry about yourself
- No comparing
- Heaven is single file
- Move at your pace, on your time

I've learned in life and work that each of us has a unique race to run that is linked to our personal passions, skills, experiences, and opportunities. It belongs to us and cannot be compared to the race being run by others. We cannot allow the stigma of judgment, comparison, or envy to tempt us off course. When we do, we violate the fullness of our unique contribution. This can short-circuit our potential. We lose sight of the end goal, and in turn, we lose sight of ourselves.

I want to encourage those of you on the path to the 4G Factor life to avoid getting caught up in comparing yourself to others. Your 4G Factor lifestyle is like your fingerprint. It is unique to you. It is what you say it is. It is what you want it to be. It is your choice. POINT, BLANK, PERIOD!!! The same qualities that bred success centuries ago are the same ones that breed success today. This wisdom never changes. Winners apply their passion and effort, knowing that if they want different outcomes, they must put in the work using the traits that bring victory.

Characteristics of Winners

Surround Yourself with Winners. - Winners evaluate the people they spend time with. The people you interact with regularly play a huge role in every area of your life. They have a direct impact on who you are or become. I'm sure you have heard the saying, "You are what you eat?" It's the same scenario. If you hang around people who challenge your thinking and way of life, you will find yourself wanting more out of life. If you hang around toxic people, you will more than likely become toxic as well. 4G Factor individuals are intentional, and every moment is important to maximize your full potential.

NEVER give up. - Throughout your day, I'm sure you will encounter people who gave up on their dreams too soon.

When you give up on something you want to achieve, you tell your brain to get into the habit of giving up. This keeps you from reaching your 4G goals, but you'll also be more likely to plant a seed of quitting and giving up that will manifest later. When you feel like giving up, remember that these are defining moments for you and your future. As I mentioned earlier, yes, the journey will appear to be lonely, and it seems like it is impossible, KEEP GOING!!! DON'T QUIT!!!. Winston Churchill said, "Never give up on something that you can't go a day without thinking about."

Work Hard and Persevere. - There is no substitute for hard work. Every 4G person will tell you they work as hard or harder than anyone else. Things don't just happen. We make them happen! We have to put in the time. Hone your craft. Hard work and perseverance.

Remain Humble. - An ego can be a destructive thing. Good things happen to good people. Humility leads to the path of the 4G lifestyle. Someone shared during a community forum I participated in that we can get things done by laying down egos and logos. That is a drop-the-mic moment! Remaining humble allows for growth. Respect yourself and others while also standing up for your values and beliefs. I said humble, not a pushover!

Possess Enthusiasm and Passion. - Nothing kills momentum and creativity faster than a humdrum person. A sour attitude is deadly to just about anything it touches. 4G projects are led by those who are EXTREMELY passionate about what you do. You should possess natural enthusiasm and passion for that thing you are pursuing. It's what calls you when you are bone tired, but you somehow find yourself working into the wee hours of the night because you are passionate about your project. I will be the first to admit that the 4G lifestyle takes A LOT, and some days, you don't feel like being "powered up," which is natural. On those days, you need to take it way down and recharge. This is necessary to keep going at the 4G speed.

Accountability- Accountable leadership is a must in a winning life. EVERYONE needs to have someone who can hold us accountable. This person is not easily intimidated by you and your success. Someone who can check on you and love you at the same time. When you screw up, you have to own it fully. These are the moments great character is built. Winning leaders always possess this trait.

4G Moment to Reflect

What 5 characteristics of a winner do you possess?

____

____

____

____

What one thing do you need to improve on?

____

____

____

____

Chapter 8

Don't Play "The Game"

On the road to greatness, things happen. I want to encourage you not to play the game. I'm referring to the blame game, the victim game, and the cutthroat game. All three games inhibit and impede your progress to gaining 4G status. When my youngest son was 3 or 4 years old, my aunt and uncle visited. My aunt corrected him for something he was doing. He looked up at her and said, "Aunt San, worry about yourself." While this statement was rude and disrespectful, it is one that we can learn from in this chapter. To avoid playing "the games," we should worry about ourselves.

When something bad happens, the first thing we want to know is, "Whose fault is it?" Wasting time pointing fingers rather than looking for solutions is usual, but it's far from constructive. The blessing and the curse of working on a 4G project is that you are the only person who should be blamed. But, somewhere down the line, we convince ourselves that it is a laundry list of things and/or people who can be blamed for our project not meeting our expectations.

If you set goals, you expect results. However, what do you do when you do not quite meet your planned mark? Do you acknowledge that the goal still needs to be met or the project failed because of you? Or do you start complaining or even blaming others for the results you got? Instead of taking ownership of the blame, we look for someone else to blame.

> **It's good to stay focused on the progress but not let the focus be solely on the results of a project.**

A great example of this is when you are losing weight. You get on the scale daily, checking how much weight you have lost. Focusing on the results rather than the progress, you become frustrated and risk aborting the goal of the entire project.

Blaming someone else or complaining about your situation doesn't take accountability. Instead, you make someone else accountable for your situation. In reality, you can't make anyone else responsible for your life other than yourself. So, if you choose to make someone else accountable, you are misleading and hindering yourself from moving on. This will keep you in a holding pattern. Staying in this holding pattern will most likely cause you to procrastinate. To break the cycle and get unstuck:

1. Stop blaming others and start holding yourself accountable.

2. When you don't get the results you want or expect, ask yourself what you have done so far to get the results you have now.
3. Ask yourself what you can do to change your behavior to get other results.

Playing the blame game also negatively triggers your mental filters. We all filter our information based on personal experiences and/or beliefs. So, instead of seeing your project as a 4G opportunity, you will focus more on the challenges and problems caused by others. This will move you further away from the real issue, which is producing greatness.

We all want to play the victim sometimes. When we choose to play the victim, we get to have our needs met without asking directly and can blame whatever isn't working on someone/something else. The victim doesn't take responsibility for their behavior or their feelings.

When you play the victim, it can feel really good. It feels good not to take responsibility or ownership for what's happening. We present the problem as if it's out of your control. This is really a cry for you to be rescued or have someone to look after you. Playing the victim game gets people off of our backs temporarily.

Much of stopping playing the victim is self-awareness. We must acknowledge our feelings and set realistic goals for where we are at the moment and what we can actually do. Setting ambitious goals is not going to be helpful! Resist the urge to self-sabotage yourself! Resist and challenge those feelings that say you're not good enough or worthy to receive joy, happiness, or success.

To thrive as a 4G person, you MUST stop blaming everyone else for what you did or did not do. Blaming other people because you don't have something will give all your power to the other person. Your project and your life are your responsibility. And it's only when you take full responsibility for those things that you actually do something about them. You can blame others as much as you like; it does not change anything. It will exercise greater judgment about what's really going on.

4G people do not get into the habit of blaming others. They understand that this will help them to become more resilient. Being resilient allows you to recognize that if you are disappointed about how your project is going, it is your responsibility to take the initiative and do something about it.

Several years ago, my company tripled in size. We hired staff and did an abridged staff orientation and training to get all the sites covered. Months later, while visiting the sites, I was not pleased with how the staff interacted with the students. I pulled the Site Coordinators aside and chewed them out for their performance. Later, when speaking to my mentor, she said, "Gretchen, whose company is this? Who is responsible for training the staff?" I was playing the blame game instead of taking responsibility for what I did not do. The following week,

I called a staff meeting. I conducted a detailed training and orientation to correct what I failed to do the first time. After the training, I was more confident about my team and how they would perform.

At this point, I removed the blame from anyone else and was now holding myself accountable. I took ownership and stopped making excuses for not going with our standard level of excellence. Making excuses is the first step to failure. Removing blame is also a way to remind you of your standards and principles. Playing the blame game is a shortcut; you avoid your standard practices. Staying true to your 4G plan allows space for personal growth. You don't focus on what went wrong, but what you can do now. This enables you to continue to develop as a person and make strides at successfully implementing your 4G project.

By ending the game, you give yourself permission to grow, be accountable, and accept responsibility for everything. Let's make a pack right now. When you can play the blame game or be the victim, your answer should be, "I retired my jersey, and I don't play those games anymore!"

4G Moment to Reflect

What do you do when you do not quite meet your planned mark?

____

____

____

____

Do you acknowledge the goal still needs to be met or the project failed because of you?

____

____

____

____

Do you start complaining or even blaming others for the results you got?

____

____

____

____

Section 3

Grind

Chapter 9

Your 4G Fingerprint

No one can tell you how to grind. This is not a one-size fits all. Everyone has their own 4G fingerprint. You can follow my example but you cannot have MY 4G. This is not the "copycat" syndrome.

I speak at this particular conference twice a year. I have been going for over 15 years now. When I first started presenting there, I was easily intimidated and concerned about people duplicating my materials, so I put my initials on every slide and every page of the handout. This particular year, I decided to sit in one of the sessions. I was given a handout when I entered the room. After being seated, I began to look at the materials, and my eyes almost popped out of my head. This lady was not only using my materials but also my EXACT handouts with my initials on them. I was HOTTTTT, but I sat there because I wanted to hear what she had to say! After listening for less than ten minutes, I began to laugh. This clown had the nerve to take my materials, but she should have studied it and me a little longer. When I tell you she was HORRIBLE, she was HORRIBLE!!! People were walking out of the session left and right. At this time, I was pissed and amused at the same time. I stayed until the session ended because I wanted to have a word with her. I approached her at the end of the session and asked if she recognized me. She said I looked familiar but wasn't sure who I was. I politely pointed to the handout and said, "I'm GDB! Enjoy the conference!"

You could learn many lessons from this story, but for the sake of this chapter, we will pick one. The lesson to learn here is that someone may have something that belongs to your 4G but cannot properly execute it because it's your 4G!

Certain things make us unique and different from anyone else. One of those things is our fingerprint. No two people or two fingers, for that matter, are the same. That pattern and print are unique to a particular person and finger.

I am a HUGE Apple fan. I think I have every iPhone, but 3 of them. I was amazed when they came up with the Touch ID. I remember my oldest son trying to unlock my phone by putting his finger on the home button. He was so frustrated because the phone would not unlock. He had done everything that he saw me do to unlock the phone, but it would not work for him. I explained that the phone would only unlock using my fingerprint because it was programmed to recognize my finger, not his.

> **Our grind is very similar to our fingerprint. It is unique to us, our project, our goals.**

No one can tell you how to grind. This is not a one-size-fits-all. Everyone has their own 4G fingerprint. You can follow my example, but you cannot have MY 4G. This is not the "copycat" syndrome. Others may try duplicating your project, but I assure you they will not get the same results.

As you think about your 4G project being unique, you must also establish what your grind looks like. You don't just get a 4G project because you are pretty or your daddy is the president of the bank. It comes with a grind   ; it is worked for, not handed to us in a trust fund from our grandparents. I can't tell you how to grind, but I will give you some suggestions on how to get STUFF done.

First, spend less time thinking about your 4G project. You have to get that information out of your head onto paper, in a notebook, or on a computer (Whatever your flavor). When information piles up in your head, it leads to stress, feeling overwhelmed, and uncertainty. Write EVERYTHING down. I keep a notepad by my bed. I can be lying in bed or dreaming even, and when I wake up, I grab a notepad to jot down things I don't want to forget.

Note-taking is the first step to exploring new or expanding projects. Consider this phase 1 of your grind. Phase 1 will make things much easier when you get to the last phase, review and execute. It's hard to review information if you do not have something tangible. You should have pages for different topics or categories to keep things organized. This will help you to find information more quickly when it is organized. This also helps you to filter out the good ideas from the not-so-good ones. This is a glorified brainstorming session. During this phase, if you have a group of trusted individuals, you may want to invite them to get into the "think tank" with you. I hear you… What's the "think tank?" The think tank is where you get your girls together with snacks, beverages, laptops, flip charts, and markers for them to help flesh out your thoughts and notes. These must be trusted individuals who will not try to talk you out of doing something or influence your project in a way you had not intended. After the think tank, review what y'all came up with to ensure that your project is still in its purest state. While reviewing, if you read anything that doesn't sit well with you or have to read more than once, don't move forward with this item. It's usually something that you are second-guessing. Please note that there is a difference between second-guessing and stretching. Stretching pulls us out of our comfort zones, while second-guessing doesn't align with our morals and beliefs.

Secondly, you must decide if the items on the list are projects, action items, or just things to know. This is phase 2. If it is a project item, name the project, create a new page, and using the list from phase 1, move all related items to that page. (Using an electronic device makes the grind easier and will help you work more effectively and efficiently.) Some of your action items may be related to this project, which will serve as deliverables and/or goals. This action item will be needed to develop your 4G project. If it is an action item, attach dates, times, tasks, and points of contact. This will help you to clearly identify what needs to be done. Set a schedule with dates for the action items to be implemented and completed. Also, prioritize your action items as to what needs to be completed first by importance and deadlines. I suck at this step. I tend to procrastinate. A helpful strategy for me is to put it on my calendar with alerts that remind me to complete the necessary tasks. Set small goals to avoid feeling overwhelmed. Accomplishing 12 small tasks is much easier to digest than one large task. Truthfully, one large task comprises many small tasks, so why not break them down.

Identify issues and complete a risk assessment. The risk assessment does not have to be formal but will weigh all factors before execution.

The last step is to review and execute. Welcome to Phase 3! This is where you turn your grind up. This is where the magic happens. Frequently look over, update, and revise your lists. At the beginning of the week, set aside time to review your lists and organize your tasks to keep running smoothly. The review helps you adapt to changes, refocus your attention, identify the next actions, and reflect on your workflow. Doing this at the beginning of the week allows you to set the tone for the upcoming week. You should plan for execution gaps. This is when things are not going so well. Your timelines or goals were not realistic/too ambitious or were unclear to your audience. Most times when executing our 4G project, we are still working a full-time job, being Mommy, cooking dinner, cleaning, etc, so you are squeezing your project in with everything else you have going on. Have I painted a clear picture of why I said this is the phase where your grind gets turned up? All the other phases usually take place during your downtime. But when it's time   , it's competing with every available moment you have or don't have. Your 4G project must push you to keep grinding even with little to no sleep and at the expense of looking stupid. This is go time. Nothing great happens without sacrifice.

Earlier, I mentioned running for office during the pandemic. Because there was no blueprint, we had to figure things out. There were late nights, Zoom calls, and multitasking at a whole different level because everyone in my family was home and could not go anywhere, so I was juggling my time with them as well. You talk about grinding, oooooooweeee!

Remember, the 4G life will open many opportunities for you, but the grinding process is not glamorous. It's downright messy. It's not always filled with applause and cheering. Believe it or not, 4G is about the small, mundane tasks that need to be done day in and day out. This is where many people struggle to stay engaged and motivated. It is the small moments during the most challenging phase that leads to producing greatness.

4G Moment to Reflect

Create your "grind plan". How will you execute your 4G project?

Chapter 10

Sharpen Your Skills

We are full of opportunities and undiscovered potential that is untapped. We have a tendency to neglect and do not invest in ourselves. Investing in yourself is one of our superpowers for anyone wishing to discover their 4G potential. YES, I'm asking you to take your money and not buy that new bag or shoes but to invest in opportunities that develop you. This investment is more than just a choice — it's necessary if you want to excel and stay at the top of your game. Self-investment is a priority and essential for your progress. It helps you unlock your full potential and shape your personal growth journey.

> **Dedicating yourself to personal development sets the stage for accomplishing great things and empowers you to lead a rewarding life.**

By investing in yourself, you lay the foundation for achieving remarkable success. Most individuals do not take the time to sharpen their skills. This is an opportunity to personally invest in who you desire to be and where you want to go. It can assist you in further developing existing skills and in learning new ones. If you are bi-vocational (working 2 jobs), it can also help you stand out amongst others in the same field; showing that you have completed professional development programs or additional certifications strengthens your resume.

Personal investment allows you to stay relevant. It keeps you up to date with trends and changes in your field. Industries constantly evolve, and new technologies, processes, and practices emerge. Professional development helps individuals stay current with these changes and competitive in their field. For instance, if you work in the tech industry, staying up-to-date with the latest software updates and programming languages is crucial to remain relevant.

I will admit that this personal investment is usually difficult for those of us who have been around awhile or are known as an "expert" in a particular area. I MAKE myself attend at least "formal" sessions a year. I say "formal" sessions because you can pick up different strategies daily when engaging with others. I recently attended a public speaking seminar. I act like I'm in school when I attend these sessions. I minimize my distractions. This means I limit my phone calls and texts because I would like to get as much as possible out of the session. I have my laptop, notebook, pens, pencils, highlighters, and snacks. The presenter was captivating from the start to the end. One would think that after conducting keynotes, seminars, and workshops for over 20 years, there is probably little that I could learn. WRONG! I learned four new strategies to include in my presentation that will keep my audience even more engaged. I decided to try a few of those new strategies with a group I train yearly to see if they would recognize any difference. Before I could ask, someone mentioned during the Q&A section that there was something different about my presentation. Once I clarified that it was a good change, I told the participants what it was. As a result of these few changes, I secured 3 new contracts!

Another way to invest in yourself is through mentorship. You will have an opportunity to gain practical knowledge and insight from someone who has "seasoned" in a particular area and has achieved the level of expertise you aspire to attain. This mentor/mentee relationship allows the mentor to have an opportunity to expand their repertoire of professional knowledge and skills through their instruction and facilitation of others. I consider mentorship one of the most valuable tools someone can have as they navigate life. Please note that you can have multiple mentors. You could have one for all the areas in your life. If you are blessed enough, you may find one who can cross over different facets of your life. Mine serves as a spiritual, personal, and professional mentor. I also have a professional mentor.

When choosing a mentor, you want to select someone you respect, look up to, listen to, and, more importantly, someone who has experiential knowledge beneficial to you and where you aspire to go. Know that the mentor is NOT a friend. This is a person who you HIGHLY esteem. It is extremely important not to cross the lines and keep the relationship pure. This will allow the mentor/mentee relationship to be maintained and not be confused. A mentor may share things you may not always agree with but is sharing those things that will ultimately yield the desired results.

> **When you have an audience with your mentor, this is a time for you to listen, take notes, and not do a lot of talking. It's like taking a master class with an expert. Take it all in and ask as many questions as possible.**

Another helpful tip is that I find the mentee wants to be chased. It is not the mentor's job to run and chase after you. It is not their job to check in with you, but you to check in with them. They have the information you desire, so if you want it, GO GET IT! WORK FOR IT! If a person agrees to be your mentor, that says they have time for you and are willing to interrupt their schedule for you. Please note that if a person does not do this, they may not be the best mentor.

A mentor/mentee relationship is best described as servanthood. The best way to learn from someone is to be around them, observe them, and serve them. When I say serve someone, it is not the most popular thing to do, but it is the most rewarding. It will give you insight into the person whom you serve. I have served my mentor for over 20 years, and I mean SERVE. There isn't ANYTHING she can't ask me to do. The times that I have gotten the most from her were not when we were one-on-one but when I was observing her, watching her interact with others, and addressing issues. One of the most valuable lessons I learned was how to respond appropriately and address difficult issues with a firm hand but with care and concern. While my primary mentor and I have different career paths, she has taught me so much professionally due to the fact that she cares and prays for me while God gives her details about how I should navigate through life. This part has been PRICELESS! For me, having a God-fearing mentor is critically important because it aligns with my religious beliefs.

One of the craziest times for me during my mentorship was when I ran for office. My mentor coached me every step of the way, only for her to tell me on the runoff election night that she knew from day one that I would win, but she could not say anything. And that it was her job to coach and push me in areas I was afraid to go alone. The best way to describe that time was similar to when you played the blindfold leadership game where you were blindfolded and had to trust someone to navigate you without you knowing what was going to happen. It was hard, but when you truly trust your mentor, you can lean into their voice and trust the process.

My challenge for you is to find a mentor who will challenge you in an area of your life. Once you find this mentor, remember they have what you need, not vice versa. This is a prime example of "you will get out of it what you put into it."

It may not always feel good or comfortable, but stick it out and know it benefits you as you further develop your 4G strength.

4G Moment to Reflect

What are two ways you will commit to investing in yourself?

____

____

____

____

____

____

____

____

Chapter 11

Grind in Color

Don't be afraid to be outstanding in the grind. Your theme song could be, "I don't do the most, but I do a lot."

Your grind attracts the attention of others, even when you don't say a word. Become comfortable in the spotlight/ let your light shine/ pop your collar.

A differentiator is the thing that sets you apart from anyone else doing something similar to you, better known as your competitors. This gives you a perceived advantage in the eyes of your target audience. Three things give you validity in this area. You have proven results of your success, be relevant and true. It's not enough to walk around saying you are an "entrepreneur" and all you have is an EIN and an email. Please note I'm not knocking your early grind because we ALL started here. To declare your grind in color, you must have proof and results. This is not the area where you "walk by faith," this is where we can see it in your client list, profit and loss statements, and most importantly, in the bank. While I believe you can learn from those 4G people who were derailed along the way, it is much easier to heed counsel from someone with a proven track record and fruit to show. If you do not matter to your prospects, they will quickly lose interest and move on to a competitor that speaks to their issues. You can't just make up things to appeal to potential clients. This could damage your reputation. This can be aspirational; however, you MUST take SERIOUS steps to make it come true soon.

Recently, someone called my office offering to be my "coach/mentor." You should know there's a lot wrong with this just by reading my previous chapter. I felt gracious and patient that day, so I listened to what she had to say. I must admit it was quite intriguing until I asked two additional questions. I asked her how long she had been in business and who her top 3 clients were. She responded that she had been in business for 4 months and I would be her first client. Her response caused me to ask her a couple more questions. I asked her if I was recommended by someone else and how she envisioned our mentor/coach relationship to go? She said I was not recommended by anyone, but she followed me on social media and thought I would make a great first client. She also shared that she didn't know how things would work because it would be a trial-and-error type thing since I was her first client. She also said she would reduce her fees to $6000/month until she worked the cliques out! I almost cussed right then and there on the phone! If the young lady was creating websites or making clothes, I might have taken a risk on her. Not to sound arrogant, but what could a person in business for 4 months with no experience in their field possibly mentor me (someone who has been in business for more than 15 years)? That's a long shot. While a part of me wanted to "read her rights," the spirit of God rose and allowed me to share some things with her that could help her as you continue her path. I even flipped the script and offered to mentor her, but she declined.

This was one of those moments where I had to know my worth and value to not lower my success for someone else to feel comfortable. This has been a long journey for me. My girlfriends accuse me of operating in "the spirit of the downplay." For years, when people would ask me what I did, I would say, "I work for an education company." To this day, I would have preferred to be in the background, but I had to embrace that I was called to be out front. Being out front exposes you and allows others to see you. Bonnie Rait said it best: "Let's give them something to talk about." Some successful individuals either downplay their success or hype it up way too much.

As 4G people, we grind that we owe it to ourselves to find that middle ground to properly expose our greatness. It is a splash of confidence. Humility, and HECK, YEAH, I DID THAT! You owe this to yourself for staying on the path to greatness. This is your reward for making it through the first 3 Gs. You don't make it through the first three Gs without quitting at least once a week or feeling like you will never reach a point where you are making significant progress. But if you stick to your grind, you will see that it is the pursuit of quality and excellence.

> **Any task worth doing is worth doing well.**

Grinding at this level motivates you to go above and beyond to deliver the highest possible quality. This commitment to excellence pushes you to continually improve your skills and knowledge, ensuring that you are constantly striving for better results. This is the epitome of grinding in color. While others will think you are doing the most, you whisper to yourself, "I don't do the most but I do a lot!!!" That a lot is what makes you 4G. That a lot is what will take you from being bi-vocational (working 2 jobs) to living your dream by pursuing your 4G project full-time. It brings in consistent PAYING clients and gets people's attention.

Grind recognizes grind! I gained insight into a popular line from the movie The Five Heartbeats. A character named Flash said, "It's lonely at the top." I believe it's only lonely at the top either because we do not take anyone with us or no one is willing to grind consistently to stay at the top. Please understand that I am not insisting that you don't take breaks or time off from work. What I am saying is that you have to have a consistent pursuit. That consistent pursuit will separate you and connect you with like minds. These like minds are in word and in deed. Many folks will talk a good game and make you believe they own a Fortune 500 company all by themselves. Most of the time, people grinding at 4G levels do a lot of talking, but they are always in learning mode. They attend events not to say they were there or for the selfies (which is ok. I love me a good selfie!), but they are there to see what new thing they can learn that will continue their path to greatness.

Grinding in color is a fundamental aspect of who 4G individuals are professionally motivated. This mindset drives 4Gers to always give our best effort, push ourselves to our limits, and strive for excellence. Grinding in color positively impacts your professional reputation, influences others, and fuels you to continuously learn and grow. Ultimately, grinding in color will set you on the path to greatness.

4G Moment to Reflect

List two takeaways you plan to implement after reading this chapter.

Chapter 12

Don't Forget About What You Already Know

It's really easy to focus on how far you have to go rather than how far you've come. Life reminds us that there are hills to climb and emotional hurdles still to come. But every now and then, you need to stop and remember how far you have come and the victories you have won. My pastor refers to it as rehearsing your victories. Sometimes, I literally sit down with a pad and paper and count my blessings. It helps me take one more step, one more breath, and last one more sunrise to sunset. It seems so easy to recant all the bad things not going right, but when you pause to recall all the progress we have made, pushing through every G until we FINALLY arrive at the final G, GREATEST.

I came across one of Miley Cyrus's songs and the chorus says,

"There's always gonna be another mountain
I'm always gonna wanna make it move
Always gonna be an uphill battle
Sometimes I'm gonna have to lose
Ain't about how fast I get there

Ain't about what's waiting on the other side
It's the climb."

This song is about the self-defeating voice we all hear at times inside our heads, and the importance of believing in yourself when you face a challenge. It's about the reality that we sometimes fail, and that life is as much about the journey as it is crossing the finish line. This is a crucial message for all of us, and especially women, to hear. We often times put the standards in place then talk ourselves out of going for it. Forgetting how many other obstacles we have overcome in the past.

Progress is progress. No matter how big or how small. I want you to celebrate you because you deserve to be celebrated. You deserve to recognize that you have overcome so much and are still here today, fighting, pushing, and not giving up. We all have past experiences that have shaped who we are today. Some of these experiences have been positive, while others have been negative. But no matter what, our past experiences have helped us to learn and grow.

Life is full of lessons, both good and bad. The good lessons help us to grow and learn, while the bad lessons help us to avoid making the same mistakes in the future. Learning from our life lessons makes us wiser and more resilient. We are better equipped to handle whatever life throws our way.

Life is a journey filled with experiences that offer valuable lessons. From childhood to adulthood, we accumulate wisdom through triumphs, failures, and everything in between. However, in the midst of the chaos of everyday life, it's easy to lose sight of these fundamental truths. We must recognize the importance of remembering and applying the life lessons we've already acquired.

Life is always teaching us lessons on empathy, perseverance, and many other valuable traits. Many times, we are so busy focusing on trying to move forward that once we have moved, we forget to stop and remember what we learned while we were moving. This oversight not only diminishes our personal growth but also deprives us of the opportunity to live more purposefully and authentically. Every encounter, whether joyful or challenging, presents an opportunity for learning.

> **Life lessons serve as the building blocks of character development, fostering emotional intelligence and resilience.**

They teach us about ourselves, others, and the world around us, providing insights that transcend superficial experiences. How many of you remember your first heartbreak and how it made you feel? Do you also remember what that heartbreak taught you? When we acknowledge and internalize these lessons, we have a deeper understanding of ourselves and our place in the world. Life lessons shape our perspectives, influencing how we interpret and respond to the world. They serve as lenses through which we view our experiences, informing our beliefs, values, and priorities. Our perspectives are not fixed but evolve over time as we integrate new insights and experiences. By revisiting and reflecting on our life lessons, we gain clarity and perspective, enabling us to navigate life's complexities with greater wisdom and purpose.

One of the most important things we can do is to learn from our past experiences. This means taking the time to reflect on what happened and to identify the lessons we can learn from it. We can also use our experiences to help us become better people. Everyone makes mistakes, but it's what we do with our mistakes that matters. We can either dwell on them and let them hold us back, or we can learn from them and move on. When we learn from our mistakes, we become wiser and more capable. We are less likely to make the same mistakes again and can better avoid future problems. Take some time to think about the things that have happened to you. What lessons can you learn from those experiences? How have they shaped who you are today?

Another important thing we can do is to forgive ourselves for our past mistakes. Holding on to guilt and shame will only keep us from moving forward. When we forgive ourselves, we can let go of the past and focus on the present. We can also start to heal from our past experiences and move on with our lives. Holding on to guilt and shame will only hold you back from moving forward. Forgive yourself for your mistakes, and learn from them to avoid repeating them.

An additional important life lesson is to be grateful for what we have. There are always people who have less than we do, and we should be thankful for what we have been fortunate enough to receive. When we are grateful, we are happier and more content. We are less likely to focus on the negative things in our lives and more likely to appreciate the good things.

When we learn from our past experiences, forgive ourselves, and be grateful for what we have, we can move forward with our lives and make progress toward our goals. We can become the best versions of ourselves and live lives full of joy and fulfillment. There will be times when you want to give up. But don't give up. Keep going, and eventually, you will achieve your goals.

We should always strive to be the best version of ourselves. We should never give up on our dreams and always look for ways to improve ourselves. When we strive to be our best, we are happier and more successful. We are also more likely to positively impact the world around us.

Life is a journey, and there will be ups and downs. But learning from our life lessons can make us wiser, happier, and more successful. We can make a positive impact on the world around us, and we can leave our mark on history.

Making progress from your past experiences is not easy. It takes time, effort, and commitment. But it is possible. By following these tips, you can move forward with your life and create a future that is full of joy and fulfillment.

"Grinding to not pursue your dreams, but to achieve the goals that will result in the dream being manifested."

4G Moment to Reflect

What are some examples of things you have learned from your life's experiences?

____

____

____

____

____

____

____

____

Section 4

Greatness

Chapter 13

Time to Shine

Once you have mastered the first three factors of success, you are ready to embark on the journey to the last G, greatness. Greatness is not something that happens overnight. It takes time, effort, and dedication. But it is possible for anyone willing to put in the work. Once you put in the work, it feels like an eternity ago when things seemed grim and dark. It will appear to others that you got here overnight, but you know that it was a long road of challenges and triumphs.

On this road to the 4G Factor, you have achieved greatness and surrounded yourself with positive people who supported and believed in you. 4G people need people who will challenge them to be their best and help them achieve their goals. This is the time to celebrate your willingness to take risks and step outside your comfort zone. Greatness is not achieved by playing it safe.

> **4G people must be willing to take risks, try new things, and fail because failure is a necessary part of success. Greatness is only achieved with hard work and the long hours necessary to achieve your goals.**

This journey to greatness has not been easy, but it is worth it. Achieving this level of greatness changes not only our own lives but also the world around us. The 4G life makes a positive impact on the lives of others and leaves our mark on history.

Along the way, you have experienced many challenges and setbacks. But you stayed focused and committed and eventually achieved your goals. One of the most important things we can do to help ourselves is to become familiar with our growth and success.

It's important to take the time to reflect on past accomplishments. You can learn a lot about yourself. You can see what you did well and identify areas to improve. This is helpful to make better decisions in the future, and it can also help to stay motivated when things get tough.

There are many ways to reflect on our growth and success. One way is to keep a journal or diary. When we write down our thoughts and feelings, we can see patterns emerge that we might not have noticed otherwise. We can also identify our strengths and weaknesses and set goals for ourselves. I love to go back and read my old journals. My reading them usually turns into what we Pentecostals call a "praise party!" I get overjoyed reading what was a MAJOR challenge compared to my present experience.

Another way to reflect on our growth and success is to talk to friends and family. They often provide valuable insights into our lives and help us see our accomplishments in a new light. Hearing someone else recount your story is one of the most humbling experiences. I don't care how tough you are; get the tissue. I promise you will have an "ugly cry" before it's all over.

I want to challenge you to have an out-of-body experience. Let me explain before you close this book and think I have lost my mind. For one day, I want you to observe your own behavior. Pay attention to what you do and look for patterns to help you better understand yourself. Also, look for areas where you see positive change and maturity. You will be surprised by what you see.

Reflecting on our growth and success is an integral part of the journey to greatness. It can help the 4G person stay focused and motivated and help them learn from their mistakes. When we know where we have come from, we can better appreciate where we are going.

Clearly, you have a lot to celebrate. The Winans, a gospel group, sang a song that said, "Millions didn't make it, but I'm one of the ones who did." That's YOU! So many people start on the path to greatness but get frustrated, tired, and give up. THAT'S NOT YOU!

You've worked hard, you've persevered, and you've overcome challenges. You've learned from your mistakes, grown, and achieved your goals. You're ready for the next level.

This is the time to celebrate your success. This is the time to reflect on your journey and all you've accomplished. This is the time to look ahead to the future and all you can achieve.

> **You are a 4G person. You are a go-getter. You are a risk-taker. You are a visionary. You are a leader. You are a changemaker. You are a force for good in the world.**

You are not alone. There are other 4G people out there. They are your tribe. They are your support system. They are your inspiration.

Find your tribe and surround yourself with positive people who challenge you to be your best. These are the people who will help you achieve your goals and live your dreams.

The journey to greatness is not easy. It takes hard work, dedication, and perseverance. But it is worth it. When you achieve greatness, you not only change your life, but the world around you.

You are a 4G person. You are capable of greatness. So go out there and shine!

4G Moment to Reflect

Take some time to reflect on your journey and all you've accomplished. As you look ahead to the future 4G project, jot down a few of the ideas brewing in your head.

____

____

____

____

____

____

____

____

____

____

____

Chapter 14

4G is a Club

Dear 4G Member:

Welcome to the 4G Club! YOU earned your membership to be a part of a very elite group. Your accomplishment is truly remarkable and deserving of celebration. Your hard work, dedication, and perseverance have paid off in a significant way. Your commitment to excellence and your unwavering determination have set you apart and led to this well-deserved achievement, 4G status! Your journey is a testament to what can be achieved through passion, focus, and a relentless pursuit of goals. As you bask in the glory of your accomplishment, I encourage you to take a moment to reflect on the journey that brought you here. Remember the challenges you overcame, the lessons you learned, and the support you received along the way.

Your success not only reflects your own abilities but also serves as an inspiration to those around you.

So many traveled this journey with you. They have cheered you on, pushed you, and been there when you thought you were crazy and falling apart. This is your trusted, closest group of friends and family members. I know you want to bring them into the club with you, but this is a members-only club, meaning your loved ones will have to travel their path to greatness. I live by the philosophy that it's only lonely at the top because you don't invite anyone to come along with you. But even if you take someone with you, they still have to earn their membership privileges just like you did. The difference with you is that they know someone "on the inside" who can coach them through the path, avoiding some of the pitfalls and mistakes you made.

> **As a side note, please steer clear of trying to make someone become a member who is not interested or ready. You don't want to risk your membership for someone who is not ready.**

This is usually hard for most because you feel like you are leaving your crew, and they may even accuse you of changing or thinking you are better than them. Those comments often stem from jealousy, but I would not avoid what they are saying. I would do a good soul search to ensure you stay rooted in the person you have been destined to be. Also, note that the 4G path does change you but should not change how you treat people and make them feel.

As a member of the club, you are now exposed to different levels of people who you can learn from and who can further strengthen your 4G network. When I first earned the club, I committed everything I learned to share it with someone else to make their journey easier. I have and still do share so much with my trusted circle, and many of them are now on their path to 4G and KILLING IT!

As new a 4G member, I want to encourage you find your circle within the club, a group of people who will support you and help you achieve your goals. You want to be selective with who you allow in this circle. You want those who have a bandwidth greater than yours. You have gotten out of the walls that have contained you, and you need someone to help strengthen your 4G. As your 4G strengthens, you can bring others along with you.

When you find your circle, you'll find that you're not alone as you continue your next level of greatness. You'll have people to support you from a place of understanding because they are familiar with the journey and the path. Navigating in new circles can be challenging, but it's also an exciting opportunity. It's a chance to meet new people, learn new things, and grow.

That's why it's essential to be selective about who you let into your new circles. Only surround yourself with people who will support you and help you achieve your goals.

Leaving the pack and navigating in new circles is not easy, but it's an important part of the journey to greatness. It's a chance to grow, learn, and become the best version of yourself. Don't be afraid to take the leap. Step outside of your comfort zone and start exploring new circles. You might be surprised at what you find.

The journey to greatness is not easy, but it is worth it. The best way to achieve greatness is to surround yourself with people who will support and help you reach your full potential.

Once again welcome to the club!

Sincerely,

The 4G Welcoming Committee

4G Moment to Reflect

What are some characteristics of individuals you would like in your circle?

Chapter 15

The Journey of Greatness Never Ends

The journey of greatness never ends. It is a trip marked by continuous self-improvement, relentless pursuit of goals, and an unwavering commitment to excellence. This journey transcends time and space and faces every challenge, no matter what. Greatness is a process. It is ongoing, fueled by passion, resilience, and a quest for knowledge.

At its core, the journey of greatness is deeply personal. For many of us, it begins as a spark that ignites our soul. The 4G life propels individuals into uncharted waters, pushing us beyond our comfort zones. I liken the 4G life to the same faith that caused Peter to get out of the boat and water on water. Like Peter, you may look crazy to others, but consistently pursuing greatness requires you to fix your eyes on that thing and that thing alone.

> **The path to greatness is often characterized by perseverance and a willingness to embrace failure as a steppingstone to success.**

Failures become an opportunity for growth, a chance to refine skills, and a reminder that the journey is as crucial as the destination. In the face of challenges, resilience is tested, where the 4G person shines the brightest.

The journey to greatness is a continuous learning experience. It involves a hunger for knowledge, a commitment to self-discovery, and an openness to new ideas. 4G individuals recognize that the quest to learn more becomes the compass that guides them to the next level of excellence. They also understand the importance of seeking opportunities to expand their horizons.

It is easy to become complacent once you arrive at 4G status. You have worked so hard to get here. Now that you are here, it's easy to kick your feet up and chill. But baby, this is the worst thing that you can do. You must do the total opposite. I encourage you to take a break and do some self-care, but only for a short time. 4G   Life is not a country club or a lifetime membership organization. It is a status that you must continue to work to maintain and maximize.

I want to slow the discussion down just a bit here to say that if you are like me and have multiple projects operating in the 4G status, you must pay attention to all projects. 4G individuals are just that, 4G in all things. The 4G status is a lifestyle and behavior you don't go in and out of. Either you are, or you are not. For example, if you lose 50 pounds, you must maintain the same diet, exercise, etc., to keep the weight off. The 4G status is the same thing; you must maintain the same habits, discipline, and structure it took to get you here.

A couple of years ago, I had a lot going on personally and did not maintain my 4G habits. I initially noticed a few changes, but because I was so overwhelmed with life, I did not lock in, and things started to slip out of my grasp. While I was "in my feelings," my business was diminishing before my eyes. To date, I am still working to get back on track. I learned a valuable lesson during that time. When life happens, and sometimes it takes our breath away, we have to recognize that we can't maintain the status quo. This is a good time to tag a friend who also has 4G status and ask them to grind for us until you get to a place where you can take things back over. This is when collaboration and connection play a pivotal role in the journey of greatness. Great individuals recognize the importance of surrounding themselves with like-minded individuals, mentors, and a supportive community. The exchange of ideas and shared experiences become catalysts for innovation and personal development, propelling everyone involved further on their respective journeys.

The journey of greatness is a testament to one's capacity for growth, resilience, and excellence. It sets high standards, overcomes challenges, and constantly raises the bar. When 4G individuals reach one accomplishment, another one is already on the horizon, pushing us further on the path of greatness and to go further.

> **To maintain your club status, the journey of greatness is ongoing and never truly concludes.**

It is a perpetual cycle of self-improvement, learning, and collaboration. 4G individuals understand that greatness is not a static destination but ever-evolving and transcends the boundaries of time. The journey reveals the potential within each of us and the impact one can have on the world. The 4G lifestyle is a commitment to continuous growth and the pursuit of next-level excellence.

The 4G lifestyle of greatness is equivalent to the fourth quarter of a football game. The fourth quarter is played at a high-intensity level. It is a series of plays of controlled aggression by a team all trying to reach the goal of winning. As a football mom, I can tell you that although all quarters are intense and important, nothing is more so than the 4th quarter, especially when you are behind. Everything is on the line when the 4th quarter arrives.

During the 4th quarter, both teams have already seen what the offense and defense are capable of. The stakes are high on both sides of the line. This has got to be the most challenging quarter to coach. When the 4th quarter starts, many players hold up four fingers together in unison to signal to each other that it is "go time." That signal means the impossible is nothing, and it is time to dig deeper to find a way to win.

Many lessons from football can be translated into the 4G lifestyle. Like the fourth quarter, the 4G lifestyle is intense, full of passion and hard hits that ultimately lead to life-changing wins.

4G Moment to Reflect

You've now been introduced to the 4G lifestyle. Use the space below to make a list of areas of your life in which you need to grow to maintain your 4G status.

____

____

____

____

____

____

____

____

____

____

____

____

About the Author

Gretchen D. Barron is a native South Carolinian and a graduate of the University of South Carolina. Gretchen has been engaged in educational program implementation and management for nearly twenty years. She has served as a local educator, State Administrator for the 21st Century Community Learning Centers Program at the South Carolina Department of Education, and the Assistant Director of Program Development and Grants at the South Carolina Department of Juvenile Justice, a Consultant for the United States Department of Education and Office of Juvenile Justice and Delinquency Prevention.

Currently, Gretchen owns and operates GBarron Consulting, LLC where its primary function is to unveil the unlimited potential in leadership by sharing her expertise to empower others, particularly individuals and organizations seeking guidance on starting, growing, and optimizing their consulting businesses. In 2005, Barron Academy was established providing after-school programs, summer camps, and one-on-one tutoring primarily to high-poverty low-performing schools in South Carolina. Barron Academy began services with 12 students in one school district and now serves hundreds of students yearly in multiple school districts in the state of South Carolina.

In 2017, Gretchen was appointed by Richland County Council to serve as on the Board of Directors for the Greater Columbia Community Relations Council where she serves as the Education Chair. She is active in her community and serves on a wide array of executive boards including Richland County School District Title One Planning Committee for Burton-Pack and John P. Thomas Elementary Schools, The View Homeowners Association, Emerge SC participant, and Junior League of Columbia.

She has been an active member of Right Direction Church International for the past twenty years. Serving as a Minister, a Kids Town Lead Teacher, and the former Chair of The Compass Community Development Corporation.

In November 2020, Gretchen elected to Richland County Council serving District 7. She is here to serve those who do not have a voice while encouraging others to use their power and ability for the better of our community by addressing kitchen-table issues: education excellence, economic development, and an active leadership through integrity and transparency.

She is a graduate of the University of South Carolina and is a PROUD GAMECOCK!

She has coined her own personal motto, "Guts, grit, and grind produces greatness." She believes that everyone was born with purpose and vision that drives them to pursue greatness.

Gretchen enjoys a GOOD laugh and spending time with her Barron Boys, James Lionel, II and Hilton Chase.